© 2022 Tom Huth

Published by
Sungold Editions
Santa Barbara

ISBN: 978-0-9991678-9-2

My Watergate Scandal

documentary poems

by Tom Huth

Sungold Editions
2022

Contents

1972	6
The New Neighbors	8
Virgin Territory	10
Just Pretending	12
Room 634 Watergate Hotel	14
Majesty	16
Valentines	18
Dirty Words	20
Red-Handed	22
Penance	24
Confession	26

Boiling Water	28
Just Teasing	30
A Clean Start	32
Autumn 1973	34
Love Letters	36
1980	38
Betwixt	40
Three Weeks Later	42
A Love That Endures	44
Dredging Up the Past	46

1972

Muskie cries in New Hampshire
Nixon and Mao meet in Peking
Jane Fonda tours North Vietnam
Father Berrigan freed on parole
Angela Davis beats a murder rap
Burglars nabbed at the Watergate

Fifty years ago

The first hand-held
calculator goes on sale
the first compact disc
the first Eagles album
the first Egg McMuffin

The Joy of Sex
    hits the bookstores
Deep Throat
    comes to the screen
I get a vasectomy
    goodbye consequence

The
New
Neighbors

They walk past our townhouse
in a suburb of Washington
boxes in their arms
I peek through the curtains
to make out the shape
of what destiny brings

Look how she moves
  swampy sleepy
    Levis slung low
      patches on her ass
        Southern comfort
      in her voice
playful all over
  long hair flirting
    with the breeze
      I spot a housewife
        who wants to be
          a hippie

Little bags under her eyes
stormclouds of vulnerability
What are their names again?

The musky fragrance
of patchouli oil

Linda

Virgin Territory

A wildfire of suspicious origin
    kindles within me
On a flight last month to Boston
I shocked myself trying to get
the stewardess's phone number

Carnal knowledge has eluded me
a virgin when I married at 22
still clueless 8 years later
about how to love or be loved

Carol has always preferred
the beer-drinking aspects
of marriage to getting lost
in romantic entanglements

I have no subtlety to my act
can't guess how to please her
other than leave her alone

If I make a scene
    she will surrender
A couple of kids from Detroit
fumbling at the grown-up game

Just Pretending

The couple next door just like us
an older girl and 5-year-old son
marched in the same antiwar protests
newly infatuated with smoking grass
    especially me and Linda
carries their stash in her jeans
Overnight we're all best friends

One Sunday Linda hears about
an antebellum mansion for sale
big enough for two families
    A commune? Carol protests
as I pull up the driveway
It's just pretending I pretend

I climb a staircase to an attic
with a fetching four-poster bed
    then hear footsteps behind
She flops across the quilt
    Who's going to sleep here?
Any reply a risk too far
Rolls over bare-tummied
    What side do you like?
Whatever side you're on
No I can't say that
instead look out the window
They're down in the yard
    Maybe they'll go away
Fat chance

*Room
634
Watergate
Hotel*

My fingers find the
  zipper at her neck
    and race it down
      like I've done
        this before

She shimmies
her shoulders
lets it fall
    red panties
    that's all
ohgod

unbuckles my belt
pops open my 501s
    reaches down
    both hands
oh sweet Savannah

With her I know just what to do
snugging up behind at the mirror
soaping each other in the shower
    all awonder

She stands on the rim of the tub
butt to the corner toes spread wide
to put her rapture just out of reach
    until I rise to meet the challenge

Majesty

Recovering in bed later
gazing out the window
at the city of stone
the State Department
  the White House
    the monuments
      the Capitol

How can all that majesty
match what we have begun?

We laugh to see a dog
spying from a rooftop
on pedestrians below
while we nestle here
spying on all of them
Why is that so funny?
Nobody's spying on us

The original Watergate break-in
a week before the limp imitation

We stroll away arm-in-arm
without paying for the room
                bad to the bone

Valentines

She starts every morning
searching for my byline
in the Washington Post
so I fashion each story
into a love song to her

I know which stony asides
will tease out her laugh
which lines in a sob story
showcase my sensitivity
Such a delight to delight
and her inspiration gives
my prose a poetic liftoff

A day after our next badness
I'm sent to cover the funeral
of an orphan so bereft no one
would pay to have him buried

Driving back to the office
I get stoned and lovely words
come raining down through
the roof of the company car

Next morning I hear the paper
slap the neighbors' doorstep
Her valentine is on Page One

Dirty Words

What an age to come of age
I keep getting assignments
about people breaking free
from routine and going off
on stupendous adventures

Each story obeys the canons
of journalistic objectivity
while celebrating my mutiny
against my well-behaved past
my lover's emancipation and
the flabbergasting glory of
this stopping-point in time

Once an uncorrupted newsman
I sneak in naughty words
to titillate my No. 1 fan
one day *snake*
   next day *shaft*
     next day *slippery*
Then she orders up words
   first an easy one *come*
     then *come together*

As Woodward & Bernstein keep
raising the stakes with Nixon
so does that Hannah with me

Red-Handed

Every Tuesday Sam leaves her the car
We meet in D.C. and hurry to a hotel
or a bushy hollow in Rock Creek Park
or a crawl space under a trendy cafe
    She keeps a blanket in the trunk

At home I'm a model husband
fixing the rickety railing
shampooing all the carpets
hoping my neighbor notices
what I super husband I am

Already she's talking soulmates
saying darling-this darling-that
    blasting our songs
    Morning Has Broken
    Here Comes the Sun
through the common bedroom wall

Driving home from work one day
    I think of my trusting kids
        think how easy it would be
           a slight turn of the wheel
               to fly off into the trees
Is that the only way out of this?

Mother's Day 2 in the morning
Sam catches us on their couch

Penance

A room in a downtown fleabag
so narrow the closet door
          swings halfway across
a dirty windowshade pulled down
to hide trash cans in the alley
a clock on the wall from a friend
to remind me time is ticking away
a dungeon designed specifically
for deserters of innocent children

    The old man next door failing
    someone rapping on his door
    Mr. Casters are you all right?

I have separated from Carol
to make this awful decision
decency?
          or dreamland?

Eight lives in the balance
Carol willing to forgive
Linda waiting for the word
staying with Sam just in case
Do all four children wonder
whose daddy I'm going to be?

    Have you fallen Mr. Casters?
    Mr. Casters?

Confession

She calls me in my cell
every weekday morning
after Sam leaves for work

Today a rough awakening
    I need to tell you
    I slept with someone
She says who
a boy of 18
    I couldn't help myself darling
    I haven't seen you in weeks
I picture her seducing him
the kid's hands everywhere
fawning fondling feasting
    Don't be angry
    I couldn't tell Sam
    He'd kill me
Should I take that as a compliment?
    It wasn't like being with you
I'm sure you didn't mind trying

But I won't shout and swear
would never raise a hand
won't let her write me off
    as just like the others

I will hold myself aloft
as the safekeeper of love
even if it ends up a curse

Boiling Water

Two months into hermitage
    the decision is made
but how can I tell Carol?

I imagine standing in her doorway
dropping off the kids one Sunday
watching her dissolve into tears
this woman who loved me as well
as she could my whole adult life

I put it off
  put it off

Linda and Sam keep it together
by partying with other couples
    (I don't press for details)
while she romances me by phone
and periodically in flagrante

She has an accident at home
spills a pot of boiling water
scalding herself
  from her stomach
    to her thighs

For a while I guess
she won't be cuddling
    with anyone

Just Teasing

Four months have passed
Mr. Casters long gone
me still paralyzed
  by riptides of lust
    oceans of guilt

Then one morning she calls
and I can finally give her
the banner-headline news

I told Carol I'm not coming back
I told her I have to be with you

A chilling silence
    It's been so long
It's a done deal sweetheart
    I never thought you'd do it

I get all formal
Linda Rountree will you marry me?

She laughs
    No
No?
    I'm just teasing
    Of course I will

What kind of joke is that?

A Clean Start

Every time she comes back to me
she begins by taking a shower
to get a clean start I suppose
or wash away I don't know what

Hair wet on the pillow later
    We'd need three bedrooms
    near the kids' school
We'll look whenever you're ready
    Didn't we used to say
    we could live in a teepee
    as long as we were together?
We can work it out if we want to
if you want to

We've had so many
  first nights
    of the rest
      of our lives
Will this one
be the last?

In the morning
before leaving
she showers again

Autumn 1973

I pick her up at her house
drive us to a nearby woods
the leaves starting to die

    We walk hand-in-hand
    sit on a hollow log

She knows why we're here
I have fallen for Holly
given notice at the Post
We're moving west together
to take up the hippie life
It comes out as an apology

My eyes searching hers
Linda this was our dream
You were always the one
I wanted to do this with
Now I'm saying goodbye
I will never understand

Linda Linda Linda
unbuckles my belt
Linda Linda Linda
pops open my 501s
    slips a hand in

I'm sorry sweetheart
is all I can summon

Love Letters

I miss you darling
but so many years have passed
I carry you around inside me
I don't want to disturb what
you and Holly have in Colorado
  but I cannot forget
    the brilliant light
      we created together
I still see your light dear Tom
I always say this when I write
but I'd so love to see you again

Tonight is blanket-cool in Virginia
I'm in bed alone stoned and snuggly
incense burning on my bedside table
crickets and whippoorwills jamming
an owl hooting from the woods like
an Indian calling out to his sister

My mind plays over the piano keys
of memory and the song is of you
Last night I dreamt you were here
We embraced and got into a frenzy
The moment you entered me darling
I had an orgasm that woke me up
    I was glowing all over
    We met on another level
      I am sure of it

1980

Dear Linda

I thought I saw you in Gold Hill
    alas an imposter
still I felt you back in my bones

Last winter my brother was murdered
I won't get into the grisly details
but one regret still hangs over me
I hadn't seen Jerry in seven years
I called him Christmas Day to say
I wanted to visit him in Minnesota
    Three weeks later he was gone

Linda seven years have also passed
since I last laid my gaze upon you
seven years of hiding your letters
How can I chance the same mistake?

I want to come see you in Key West
I can get an assignment in Florida
Can you picture four or five days?

You might have someone else by now
but I tingle to be with you again

Betwixt

What the hell am I thinking
reaching out to my tormentress
risking my journey with Holly
my whole Colorado adventure?

Our stepfamily disjointed
stepson running the show
me feeling the outsider
I want to make certain
I made the right choice

I try to persuade myself
seeing Linda might let me
put her behind me for good
but haven't yet mapped out
how I can frolic for days
in solitary entwinement
with my vamp from Savannah
then leave with a handshake

still betwixt and bewitched

No one will ever love me
as hard as Linda loved me
Her hunger for my flesh
her delicious invitation
her flagrant provocation
    made this boy a man

*Three
Weeks
Later*

A phone call from Key West
    I'm sorry to tell you
    Linda died last night
    in a hit-and-
Gone?
    bicycling home from work
    at three in the
She's gone?
    We'll have a church service
    because her parents
Not waiting for me anymore?
    but if Linda had any religion
    it was the high-heel religion
She wore heels?
    so we'll have a wake that night
Did I even know her anymore?

I protest
I just wrote to her!

    I found the letter
    on her nightstand

What is left for me to do
but keep checking the mail?

At least she died knowing
I wanted to be with her

A
Love
That
Endures

Grief with a chaser of relief
Holly and I marry at last
one beautiful elegant woman
more accomplished than Linda
more confident more creative
more cultured more classy
more loyal
    just not as bad

Her boys go to live with Dad
leaving me in joyful straits
    alone with the princess
Together we roam the world
share 45 years of intimacy
in health then in sickness
Holly my one enduring love
another my unlived passion

Linda would have been mine
if I'd decided right away
But would it have lasted?
She fancied me the most
when I was already taken

The only freedom I wanted
    was to be with her
Her appetite proved larger
    for freedom itself

Dredging Up the Past

An old man now in my 70s
Holly dying of Parkinson's
I look up Linda's daughter
on a trip back to Washington

Michelle tells tales of tenderness
and tales of neglect about a mother
whose first need was to be desired
Michelle professes she loves me
wishes I'd been her stepfather
It would have changed everything

She shows me a photo from Key West
a woman with chopped bleached hair
    How can that be Linda?
Oh I shouldn't be snooping around

Michelle says her mom tended bar
at a gay night club where she was
idolized for her ever-playful ways

To mask my sadness I make up an excuse
In Key West she could flaunt her gifts
without being possessed or mistreated

    Still I shouldn't have come here
    playing Woodward & Bernstein
    The fantasy was so much better
    Wasn't that always our story?